LIVEWIRE CHILLERS

The Ride to
Hell

Iris Howden

Published in association with
The Basic Skills Agency

Hodder & Stoughton
A MEMBER OF THE HODDER HEADLINE GROUP

Orders: please contact Bookpoint Ltd, 39 Milton Park, Abingdon, Oxon
OX14 4TD. Telephone: (44) 01235 400414, Fax: (44) 01235 400454.
Lines are open from 9.00-6.00, Monday to Saturday, with a 24 hour message
answering service. Email address: orders@bookpoint.co.uk

British Library Cataloguing in Publication Data
A catalogue record for this title is available from The British Library

ISBN 0 340 69758 X

First published 1997
Impression number   10 9 8 7 6 5 4
Year   2005 2004 2003 2002 2001 2000 1999

Typeset by Fakenham Photosetting Ltd, Fakenham, Norfolk.
Printed in Great Britain for Hodder & Stoughton Educational,
a division of Hodder Headline Plc, 338 Euston Road, London NW1 3BH
by Athenæum Press Ltd, Gateshead, Tyne & Wear.

The Ride to
Hell

The Ride to Hell

Contents

1

Getting Out

Kath and I had just got married.

We had no money to buy a house.

So we lived with her mum and dad.

Her mum and dad were nice.

I was like a son to them.

But I wanted some fun.

It was so boring living with them.

Every night was the same.

We sat and watched TV.

They never watched the programmes

that I wanted to see.

Kath's dad fell asleep in his chair,

at the same time every night.

He slept with his mouth open.

Her mum sat and knitted.

Click, click, click, click, click.

I hated the sound.

It drove me mad.

Every half hour she would say,

'I could just do with a nice cup of tea.

Put the kettle on, Kevin, love.'

I had to get out of the house.

I went out drinking with my mates.

At first I only went on Fridays and Saturdays.

Soon I went out every night.

Anything was better than staying in.

We went to pubs near my work.

I liked *The Ram* and *The Crown* best.

We played pool or darts.

I was drinking too much.

I knew I should stop but

I didn't want to sit at home every night.

Kath wasn't happy.

She wanted me to stay in.

We'd planned to save for a house.

I was spending all my money in the pub.

She begged me to come home from work

and forget about the pub.

She didn't like my mates.

They took up too much of my time.

But I couldn't help it.

I hated staying in.

The click of the knitting drove me mad.

2

The Last Bus

One night I had too much to drink.

I stayed in the pub till late.

It was closing time.

I knew I had to hurry.

I did not want to miss the last bus.

I ran all the way to the bus stop.

No-one else was waiting.

I must have missed the bus.

Then I saw it coming.

The bus came out of the fog.

My nightmare was about to begin.

It was to be a ride to hell.

The bus was empty but for one old lady.

I paid the driver and sat down.

I fell asleep.

When I woke up the bus was full.

People had got on while I slept.

A man sat in front of me.

I looked at him.

I knew I had seen him before,

I couldn't think where.

Then it came to me.

He had been on the TV news.

He had died in a fire.

'Hang on,' I told myself,

'He can't have died! He's on this bus!'

The back of his neck was red.

It was red with scars like burns.

Near me was a woman.

I felt I had seen her before,

a long time ago.

Then it came to me, she was Dot.

Dot was my mother's friend.

She was killed in a car crash.

I was ten at the time.

I began to feel afraid.

The bus stopped and a man got on.

It was my Uncle John.

My Uncle John died last May.

I knew it was him.

I was sure this time.

He wore the same old coat.

The same flat cap.

He had the same pipe in his mouth.

Now I felt very scared.

All the people on the bus were dead!

I went up to speak to Uncle John.

I had always liked him.

He would never do me any harm.

'Hello, Uncle John,' I said.

But he didn't answer.

He looked right through me,

As if I wasn't there.

'Uncle John,' I said, 'It's me, Kevin.'

My uncle just sat staring.

I felt his hand.

It was as cold as ice.

Things went from bad to worse.

I turned and came face to face with a skeleton.

My heart was thumping.

I went cold all over.

The skeleton was hanging from a rail.

Its hands gripped the rail.

It moved from side to side.

It had a horrible grin on its face.

I saw a badge pinned to its ribs.

The badge said KEVIN.

I wanted to scream but no sound came out.

I closed my eyes and pushed past it.

3

Stop!

I ran off down the bus,

I was shouting at the top of my voice.

I rang the bell.

'Stop the bus,' I shouted.

'Next stop driver, please.'

I ran to the front of the bus.

But there was no driver there.

His seat was empty.

The bus was driving itself.

The bus was going fast.

It was hard to stand up.

I had to hold on to a rail.

The other people just stared ahead.

No-one moved.

They sat still as if made of stone.

Their faces were pale.

The skeleton moved from side to side.

It seemed to be coming closer.

I looked out of the window,

I did not know where we were.

I had never been to this part of town.

By now I was shaking with fear.

How could I be here?

On a bus full of dead people.

With no driver.

In a strange place.

With a skeleton coming closer?

Had I also died?

Was I on my way to hell?

I told myself that was rubbish.

Of course I was still alive.

But I had to do something.

I had to stop the bus and jump off.

I moved into the driver's seat.

I took hold of the wheel.

I put my foot hard on the brake.

I braked hard.

But nothing happened.

I tried again.

The bus did not slow down.

The fog was getting worse.

It was thick and grey.

It was hard to see the road in front.

Then all at once I saw something.

It was something I knew.

The bus shelter at the end of my street.

Someone stood there waiting.

It was Kath, my wife.

She had come to meet me.

I hit the brakes again.

This time they worked.

The brakes gave a loud scream.

The bus skidded on the wet road.

Right in front of us was the shelter.

I was going to kill my wife.

I shut my eyes. I waited for the crash.

Then I felt a hand on my shoulder.

I jumped up with a start.

I looked around.

I was back in my own seat.

The driver was back in his.

An old lady was standing over me.

She had woken me up.

The rest of the bus was empty.

'Wake up, dear,' she said.

'You'll miss your stop!'

I thanked her and said goodnight.

I got off the bus.

Kath came out of the shelter.

She gave me a kiss.

'I was worried about you,' she said.

'You are so late. What happened?'

'It's a long story,' I said.

I was still shaking with fear.

It had been a very bad nightmare.

'I'll tell you about it one day.'

4

Change

I'm too afraid to stay out now.

The nightmare never goes away.

I think about the people I saw.

I can't get the skeleton out of my mind.

Why did the badge have my name on it?

Why did the others look like real people?

Will I die soon?

Kath is pleased that I stay in now.

We've nearly saved enough for a house.

I've changed a lot.

I still can't tell her what happened on that bus.

All I know is that I was on a ride to hell.